Artistic Alchemy

Artistic Alchemy

Transmuting Cinnabar into Gold

Ken Bazyn

RESOURCE *Publications* · Eugene, Oregon

ARTISTIC ALCHEMY
Transmuting Cinnabar into Gold

Resource Publications
An Imprint of Wipf and Stock Publishers
199 W. 8th Ave., Suite 3
Eugene, OR 97401

www.wipfandstock.com

PAPERBACK ISBN: 978-1-5326-3451-2
HARDCOVER ISBN: 978-1-5326-3453-6
EBOOK ISBN: 978-1-5326-3452-9

Manufactured in the U.S.A.   OCTOBER 12, 2017

Contents

Preface

A Whisper

Our life is but a whisper
amid the screaming world.

Acknowledgments

DEEP PRAISE IS DUE to my wife, Barbara, with whom I had delightful tête-à-têtes on the meaning of these poems, so raising their levels, and to David Reynolds, who never seems to tire of improving my style, grammar, theology, and the overall impression a book can make.

My gratitude spills over to Wipf & Stock for continuing its commitment to publishing worthy Christian poetry and to Kyle Lundburg for exceptional typesetting skills.

Thanks, too, belong to Robert Meier for developing my film and making such wonderful prints. Also, I should commend Rockbrook Camera in Omaha for putting my negatives onto a CD.

I shouldn't forget family, friends, teachers, and neighbors, who had to endure my "creative" eccentricities.

Credit is given here for first publishing the following poem:
"My Mystic Eclogue" in *Old Hickory Review*

Introduction

Bearing a New Song into Your Presence

A "CHARACTERISTIC COMMON TO God and man," mystery writer Dorothy Sayers declares, is "the desire and ability to make things."[1] In the book of Genesis, creation is not a one-time event, but a continuous, ongoing process. God did not wind up the world like a clock, as many eighteenth-century Deists insisted, then let it tick away on its own.[2] Rather, God is always creating, sustaining, preserving, animating, and coaxing his universe into fruitfulness. Augustine posited that if God did not exert his creative will at each and every moment, the universe would simply collapse.[3] "All creatures are balanced upon the creative word of God, as if upon a bridge of diamond," notes the Russian Orthodox theologian Philaret of Moscow; "above them is the abyss of divine infinitude, below them that of their own nothingness."[4]

The ultimate philosophical conundrum, according to seventeenth-century German thinker Gottfried Leibniz, is "Why is there something, rather than nothing?"[5] Multiplicity, instead of zero? Or, as William James boldly asserts, "from nothing to being there is no logical bridge."[6] Christians believe that God gave birth to the universe *ex nihilo*. He did not stir

1. Sayers, *Mind of the Maker*, 34.

2. Charley, "Deism," 290.

3. Augustine, *On Genesis*, 296–97; cf. Polkinghorne, *Faith of a Physicist*, 75.

4. Lossky, *Mystical Theology of the Eastern Church*, 92.

5. Parkinson, *Leibniz: Philosophical Writings*, 199; cf. Kolakowski, *Why Is There Something Rather than Nothing?*, 114–22.

6. James, *Some Problems of Philosophy*, 40; cf. Holt, *Why Does the World Exist?*, 30.

together a brew of pre-existing matter; no, he invented time and space, setting the great chain of being into motion—stretching from amoebas to primates. In *The Chronicles of Narnia*, C.S. Lewis has the lion, Aslan (who stands for Christ), sing the land of Narnia into existence. With "gentle, rippling music," he made the valley "green with grass." From the "deep, prolonged notes" of the creator, "a line of dark firs sprang up on a ridge . . . And when he burst into a rapid series of lighter notes," primroses began "suddenly appearing in every direction."[7]

Second-century theologian Irenaeus draws on a quite different metaphor to describe creation. He refers to the Son and Holy Spirit as the "hands of God." By this, he meant that God needed no tools external to himself to accomplish his work. The Son and the Spirit, who are so very close to the Father yet still distinct from him, resemble the two hands of a human being.[8] With these bare hands, as it were, God formed the entire cosmos—everything we see and all that we do not even know how to detect. Think, for instance, of angels or the modern scientific notion of "dark matter."

In Genesis, God calls, fashions, distinguishes, and names a broad assortment of elements—sun, moon, stars, seas, land, birds, fish, and creeping things. This universe, with its billions of worlds, stretches in every known direction; the findings of modern astronomy even indicate that it is actually expanding. "And if God's incomprehensibility does not grip us," insists the great Catholic theologian Karl Rahner, "if it does not draw us into his superluminous darkness, if it does not call us out of the little house of our homely, close-hugged truths . . . we have misunderstood . . . the words of Christianity."[9] Or, as nineteenth-century American actress Charlotte Cushman declares, "[W]hen God conceived the world, that was Poetry; he formed it, and that was Sculpture; he colored it, and that was Painting; and then, crowning work of all, he peopled it with living beings, and that was the grand, divine, eternal Drama."[10]

Each of us is an actor in God's great play. But I am afraid that he did not give us a script to memorize; instead, he encourages improvisation. In fact, a number of the great discoveries in history appear to have been accidents. *Serendipity* is a word coined by Horace Walpole to depict that happy condition of someone who fails to find what he originally sought, yet, in the

7. Lewis, *Magician's Nephew*, 123, 126.

8. Hill, *History of Christian Thought*, 28; cf. Irenaeus, "Against Heresies," 487–88.

9. Rahner, *Theological Investigations, Vol. IV*, 359.

10. Clement, *Charlotte Cushman*, 53.

process, stumbles upon something just as good or even better.[11] This was based on what happened to the heroes in the old Persian fairy tale, "The Three Princes of Serendip."[12] But to experience serendipity, we must ever be vigilant, with our eyes wide open. One is reminded of the lad who was called upon to read aloud in class. After the teacher had thanked him for his elocution, she asked if he would kindly explain what he had just read. "I don't know," he mumbled, "I wasn't listening."[13]

Fortunately, there *are* moments when God makes us acutely aware. "Everybody knows such occasional hours or days of freshened emotional responses when events that usually pass almost unnoticed, suddenly move you deeply," notes novelist Dorothy Canfield, "when a sunset lifts you to exaltation, when a squeaking door throws you into a fit of exasperation, when a clear look of trust in a child's eyes moves you to tears, or an injustice reported in the newspapers to flaming indignation, a good action to a sunny warm love of human nature, a discovered meanness in yourself or another, to despair."[14]

Each day I take time for prayer and reflection on Scripture, while also making sure to do some form of aerobic exercise, like jogging, and devote at least thirty minutes to some special project I am working on, whether it is writing, photography, or another pursuit. Over time, these small creative bursts do add up.

Popular notions of creativity focus on the dramatic and seemingly spontaneous. Mozart could hear and visualize entire symphonies and even scenes from operas in his head.[15] Beethoven, on the other hand, jotted down fragments of themes in his notebooks, which he labored over for years. Critics are still amazed that masterpieces could arise out of such clumsiness.[16] I know my first draft is generally pathetic, as is often the second and third. Still, I keep pecking away. In the surge of creative excitement, I believe each new piece is the best I have ever penned. Within a few days, the awful truth sinks in, so I start again. "As I write," Christian poet Luci Shaw

11. Pickering, *Captives of the Sun*, 232.

12. Hendrickson, *Facts on File Encyclopedia Word and Phrase*, 474.

13. Gerard, "Biological Basis of Imagination," 235.

14. Canfield, "How 'Flint and Fire' Started and Grew," 211.

15. Mozart, "A Letter [1783?]," 55.

16. Spender, "Making of a Poem," 114; cf. Stringham, *Listening to Music Creatively*, 391.

observed, "I have the sensation of being at the center of a small vortex of enlarging connections."[17]

Psychologists have discovered that there is an immense capacity for perception in each of us which has barely been tapped.[18] And it may take only a "single small seed" to set us thinking, suggests novelist Henry James:[19] a chance conversation, a story read, a painting seen, a witty riposte by a friend, an illustration from a sermon, a meritorious deed observed. That seed sparks the imagination, making us, like the Psalmist, eager to "sing to the LORD a new song" (Ps. 98:1).

Would that all of the Lord's children were poets! Yet, God in his democracy has bestowed crafts and hobbies. In 1870, a pioneer woman wrote in her diary concerning her love for quilts: "I make them warm to keep my family from freezing; I make them beautiful to keep my heart from breaking."[20] As gathered believers, we can beautify God's house with floral displays, banners, woodworking, and embroidery, as well as those well-trodden paths that touch the heart: gardening and cooking.[21] "I have seen homecrafted stained glass in a Midwest village which recalled Malraux's metaphor for the art: 'A mosaic that has found its place in the sun,'" declares theologian Roger Hazelton. "I recall chalices and crosses of honest workmanship, dance dramas that were not mincing and contrived, dossal curtains that were all the more beautiful because they had been made by women of the congregation. All this is good," concludes Hazelton, "since the real enemy of style and taste in church art is the ready-made, commercial product"—which smacks of an impoverished imagination.[22]

The legendary rare-book collector, A. Edward Newton, urged young people to uncover a hobby, no, preferably two—one for indoors and one for outdoors.[23] For when a child finds something that fascinates and intrigues, he actively seeks out additional information, develops new skills, makes friends with those of a similar bent, and feels a sense of accomplishment for something well done. I remember the endless hours I spent listening

---

17. Shaw, "Beauty and Creative Impulse," 85.

18. Underhill, *Mysticism*, 56.

19. James, "Preface to *The Spoils of Poynton*," 71–73.

20. Shaw, "Beauty and Creative Impulse," 88.

21. Bauer, *Arts Ministry*. Throughout Bauer relates a number of fascinating examples.

22. Hazelton, *Theological Approach to Art*, 85–86.

23. Newton, *Amenities of Book-Collecting*, 2.

to shortwave radio as a teenager. Those voices brought me in touch with countries I had barely heard of.

What do you like to do in your spare time? How might you give that talent to the Lord or share it with others? Perhaps several people have a similar gift, so the church could form a fellowship or guild. Upon completing some noteworthy task, you may wish to exclaim with Dorothy Sayers' heroine, Harriet Vane: I "feel like God on the Seventh Day."[24] The great lyrical poet Rilke famously advised the young writer Franz Xavier Kappus: "*die Fragen selbst liebzuhaben*" and "*Leben Sie jetzt die Fragen.*"[25] In other words, love life's vexing questions; struggle and wrestle with them until you live into the answers. We have the bedrock of Scripture and church teaching; now let us also use them as a springboard for every kind of worthwhile project.

"Well! We are all *condamnés* [condemned]," nineteenth-century art critic Walter Pater once wrote, "as Victor Hugo says: we are all under sentence of death but with a sort of indefinite reprieve—*les hommes sont tous condamnés à mort avec des sursis indéfinis*: we have an interval, and then our place knows us no more. Some spend the interval in listlessness," Pater continues, "some in high passions, the wisest—at least 'among the children of this world'—in art and song. For our one chance lies in expanding that interval, in getting as many pulsations as possible into the given time."[26]

It is our calling, adds French Protestant theologian Gabriel Vahanian, to "wait without idols."[27] Perhaps we have become embroiled in lifestyles of pleasure that poison everything we touch or have developed habits of acquisitiveness, so that we are living high on the hog at expense of others' well-being. Now is the time to re-examine our bearings, set our priorities straight. In the harsh words of Jesus, you should figuratively cut off your hand, pluck out your eye, or amputate your foot—if such appendages prevent you from rejoicing in the truth.[28]

Father of lights, stir up those gifts and talents deep within us, that through patience and determination we might bring them to fruition in

---

24. Sayers, *Gaudy Night*, 199–200.

25. Rilke, "Brief 4," 18–19; cf. Rilke, *Letters to a Young Poet*, 35.

26. Pater, "Conclusion to *Studies*," 529; cf. Pater, *Studies in the History of the Renaissance*, 120.

27. Vahanian, *Wait Without Idols*. This is a quote from the chorus in section 5 of W.H. Auden's "For the Time Being: A Christmas Oratorio."

28. Blumhardt, *Action in Waiting*, 168–9.

your good time. Give us a sense of excitement in this adventure of living for you. Fertilize our imaginations, so that we become co-creators in the ongoing kingdom of grace. May we come, at last, bearing a new song into your presence.

Have Done with Donne

Have done with Donne, entomb Eliot,
Baudelaire's music box and Keats's nightingale,
decapitate Villon, string up Goethe,
spatter Yeats's blood on the doorposts of Ferdowsi.

Misconstrue thy neighbor,
slay the ghosts of giants,
worship your own creative juices,
empathize with protoplasm.

Each poet strikes chaos
with Aaron's rod that buds,
is baptized with a holy gush,
initiated into the sanctum of love.

Crashaw's farfetched angel figures,
Shelley's flowery vapidism,
Pope's incessant satirizing—
leave me cold and counteracting.

I prefer two polished stones,
ocean-whipped, to those
rough-hewn from quarries:
Dickinson to D.H. Lawrence.

Words scraped and enameled,
varnished twice, ensconced
in pulp, Bodoni Bold
or Franklin Gothic.

Imagination loosed in cadence or rhyme,
dumb ox harnessed to a Chomsky mill,
impersonating narrative,
making experience the fodder of dreams.

Bludgeoning one's friends into caricatures,
tweaking our enemy's nose,
we are the spigot of collective unconscious,
the whistle on the anthropoid stew:

réchauffé—soufflé.
(Poetry is a little house
with only room for three,
I climb in the front window,

who stole my parchment and my public?)
Keep good company—go to the Louvre.
Put nature in a pretty dress
then Cartier-Bresson her,

or bathe the nymph like Fellini
in a phantasia colorama.
Tune the syllables like a Stradivarius,
shock, if it's deemed necessary.

Peep through keyholes with the voyeur,
critique the texture, fuse style and form,
vary the mood,
depending on your philosophy.

Verisimilitude's as useful as a clean-shaven Medici,
a crooked stairway as true as the straightest banister,
like Humpty Dumpty
wrestle the word into a half-nelson
—an inscape epiphany.

A Minor Manifesto

Compress, compress.
Make each vowel count.
Unleash layers of textured meaning.
Enunciate till accents no longer clash/elide.
Be spare. Weed out what's unnecessary.
Stand aphoristic, mythic, concise.
Elaborate on couched symbols
till type and antitype reverberate.

Does each detail add to, clarify,
heighten, or resolve the tension?
Even if non-mimetic,
are the possibilities real?
Are the characters ambiguous, human to the core
or veiled vehicles of propaganda?
Are the metaphors pregnant, indeed overdue,
or have they been transposed so often,
that only erudite doctors skilled in the arcane
see beyond their primary implications?
Are the similes too taut, stretched so thin
that they fail to fill in their meaning circles?

Are the tunes sonorous, jarring?
Does one note play hard against its fellow?
Are the rules so fanatically applied
that the resulting formula is artificial, ethereal?
Are the meanings symbolist flights

of self-inebriation?
Is the language odd, memorable,
the vocabulary regional, archaic, intense?
Does the pace vary from lullaby to cubist disorder?
Are the situations vivid, percolating up from the subconscious,
spanning or breaking genre?

Is the whole unencumbered, saturated with you,
or have the plots been cribbed from some ancient primer?
Are the allusions of heroic importance,
the classics jammed with modernist assumptions?
Have you bequeathed to the world a Trojan horse
or a Pandora's box that ought to be swiftly nailed shut?
Will centuries hence pilgrims
be circumnavigating your Ka'ba stone?
Or will your fitful drafts be subsumed
under the edifice of a later, full-blown synthesizer?

Have you gone with your strengths,
shored up your flaws?
Or is there an uneven tear
straight from the prelude to the sagging finale?
Will this be another near-masterpiece
or that once-for-all incarnation
wherein the Muses sum up your peculiar era?
Strive to enter into that hallowed rest
of the oft-quoted, cross-referenced anthology—
wherein your name will be immortalized in the graffiti of schoolboys
and your acid-free papyrus preserved in Alexandrian think tanks.

The Land of Make-Believe

Labyrinths leading to minotaurs,
keys unlocking gates of oblivion,
lights dispersing foaming chaos,
shadows providing the substance for our dreams.

I walk despondent in the Land of Make-Believe
among fairies and fauns and talking trees,
the Child cemented over by the Man—
slain by the increments of time.

Flicker of the divine snuffed out
by mildew and spider webs,
serendipity suffocating under melancholia,
eloquence strangled by sophist's rhetoric.

Clio, Thalia, Erato, and Calliope
lie untapped under pointed dunce's cones,
competition or cooperation too severe,
foolish fears accepting our second-best.

We're digging ruts so deep
it will take three generations to escape,
dazzled by neophyte brainstorms,
curiosity squelched due to ecstasy.

Surprise but the first stop
in the assembly line of enchantment,
perspire for the long run;
sprinters grow old before they're twenty-five.

Cut the stultifying ropes of economic security.
Fantasize now—and then.
Generate as much chaff as wheat.
Perceive odd new relationships.

Let the concoction sit. Pour on
every fertilizer known to man.
Visit uncharted realms. Meditate.
Make yourself a symbol.

Poetic Diction

I lost something I thought I had found,
namely my sense of proportion,
a balance between prayer and work,
contemplation and creative bursts,
rough drafts and the finale.

Which medium to arbitrate
burning images and taut language
with a spark of the way-out,
to utter "I" or "thou" or "we"
via narrative, description, or conversation.

Shall I sound learned, astute,
or recite compound Anglo-words?
with syntax straightforward as Campion
or tortured, metaphysical as Crashaw?
refer to mythic heroes or just our frail contemporaries?

Autobiographical? understated? in an exuberant
or lethargic mood? using exempla drawn from nature?
the economy of Dickinson? Rilke's lyrical
tact? the booming voice of Shakespeare?
half-rhyme or blank verse?

Quotations far-flung? stanzas *ottava rima*?
Greco-Roman or Judaeo-Christian antecedents?

where the forks divide, I stand
parabolic, confused, thus I venture
foolish-warily down every path I can.

Pretend

The curtain parts and we make-believe it's real,
puppets banter and take their bow,
wobbly marionettes hang together to take the trapdoor down,
ventriloquists transplant their voice boxes into imbeciles,
Marilyn Monroe appears as Cinderella,
Jimmy Stewart, a bumbling, small-town loser,
a daub of paint and we'll make Howard Hughes a clown,
a cosmetics kit and a drunken sailor wears a crown,
if we lie in art, should we wonder at history?

Paradise

On the medieval stage
    Paradise was a raised platform
hung round with curtains and prop shades,
    Adam and Eve from their shoulders up
were half-eating citrus fruit,
    and if you cupped your hand to the wind,
you might hear the sobbing of God.

In the Circle of Light

In the circle of light
against the dark stage
when we find something spontaneous
has been carefully rehearsed,
life's spectacle dims.

The protagonist's dialogue is disingenuous,
his gestures stilted and crude,
the audience's laughter is taped
and in sync; then you question
what's myth and what's real.

Is the self and the role one?
am I the hero or villain
in the fable I wrote?
is the costume and wig mine
or am I miscast in the wrong historic age?

A prisoner of the Globe,
I'm pulled about by Plutarch and Plautus,
the pageantry of kings,
my face is a chalked mask,
my wrinkles darkened and creased.

So, I've rocked my own cradle,
I've wept over my hearse,
like the gardens of Versailles

all my edges are clipped,
my fountains controlled.

In the midst of my performance
out jump Prospero and Lear,
a prompter's cue fails,
I search for an answer,
but it's mostly gibberish I've spoken.

Homo Hypocrites

The actors and their painted faces
remind me of mine own hypocrisy,
how many masks within my wardrobe!

When all do purr before my jests,
I parade the buffoon or wit,
when among alumni or professors,
I recall my Greek or German,
downstage with those blue-collar folk
I rebut executives and politicians,
yet if legislative favor I desire,
how flattering my mouth!

In the office I rattle off statistics
with an eye toward next year's bonus,
and should a sensual urge arise,
my wife is overwhelmed with my vocabulary.
To a son I am the all-wise father,
dispensing aphorisms and reinforcement,
yet should the neighbor children visit,
I'm aloof and somber in my study.

Before the priest I quote my testaments,
to natural man, the reasoning of Aristotle.
I change my costume from work to home to play,
in the spotlight an author,
backstage a prop or cosmetics man.

Life has so many bits and parts,
we actors try each one for size,
critics hand in their notices,
then we're either cut or cast for a new performance.

One final curtain call,
all masks will topple,
we begin our title role
with a supporting cast of thousands.

In the Middle, Fabulous Kingdom

In the middle, fabulous kingdom
between the land and air,
fauns, centaurs, sylvan nymphs
retain a marginal, dream-like status,
fairy princesses are cuddled up beside ivory unicorns,
sirens shake and strum their sistrum nipples,
mermaids and mermen belly-float beside Leviathan,
Saracen candy towers are hidden in the dense undergrowth
of snapdragon lilies and hippogriff cypress,
a giant's glove can be as huge as a banquet hall,
a dwarf's scarf folded up within a thimble,
—grisaille peepholes, flying pygmies—
the mizmaze floor churns your stomach dizzy, woozy,
the bird of paradise's plumage flutters down
in a tickertape extravaganza of bantamweight flounce.

Apparent blood gushes up from underground fountains,
near its zenith instantly freezing
into a crescendo of hybrid tea roses,
the cockatrice's tongue is wound in a clove-hitch knot
by some Puck or Robin Goodfellow,
ask directions from a magnetic boulder,
whitecap clouds function as bellhops or taxis,
subconscious fears can be traced on onion paper,
scribbled out by guileless children,
hues can be shaken up and down—from grotesque to sublime—

and should you sometimes think of the good, the chances are
you may rescue fair Guinevere after three-dimensional combat
with symmetrically-opposed ogres,
and you'll find yourself pregnant, the fomenter of elves.

The Glass Flowers

The glass flowers are too delicate for me to touch,
like the world of Parmenides
or the *primum mobile,*
a Tao stillness punctures that isle of bliss,
Christ, our resurrected icon, or the statues of the Pure Land sect,
Plotinus cross-woven with Pseudo-Dionysius,
beyond Shangri-La the seven sleepers rest,
freeze-action romance and chivalry abound,
the mind paints still-life millenarian fruit
and all alchemical equations cancel each other out.

Miniature Illusions

To encase life inside a gem
in a dangling, glowing eye-catcher
whose cross-cut texture
is suffused with opal rainbows,
dispersed by metallic pyrotechnics,
like a starburst chameleon
revolving in bubbled amber,
the night sky is shrunk
to fit inside a platinum inset
of cat's-eye chardonnay or tear-shaped Bordeaux,
the cleavages run parallel in octahedral directions,
as though gazing into a millefiori well
or rubbing a rutile bottle,
as when ice ballerinas take a mist-colored spin:
a dazzling, serpentine performance
before a hall of beveled mirrors,
their transparent symmetry
refracted in cut-flower, profuse vials,
imperfections are ironed out
in a pool with no undulating ripples
whose depth is measured by micro-calipers.

Transmuting Cinnabar into Gold

Today I'm transmuting cinnabar into gold
with a majestic wave of my alchemical hand,
retrieving the stolid, leftover precipitate,
then pounding, kneading, shaking it
to procure delectable honey,
so that Lazarus levitates above his stinking tomb,
the ivory Galatea takes up Pygmalion form.

I want my bread never to stale,
but germinate till my lips turn magenta,
how inconceivable to intermingle with these myopic drones,
while my effervescent, popping companions
grasp opportunity by its sequined throat,
till it yields a portfolio of collectible artifacts.

Some scrounge about
like mad spelunkers in a mineralized netherworld,
I and my friends, however, are as uninhibited as shooting stars
who bound and careen across the open stage;
if you please then, Father Elijah,
your mantle and a double portion of your spirit,
that I may perform ritual sleight-of-hand,
for this muted landscape is intemperate with innovation.

A Surrealist Manifesto

I want to write a poem so wrenching
it will strangle and suffocate you in your chair.

A Futurist Declaration

I want to write a poem as hypnotic
as a flywheel or a rotating crankshaft.

"Stairway of Surprise"[1]

Mounting to paradise on the stairway of surprise,
little Emily exploded herself to bits,
fragments of crystal, charred metaphors,
like da Vinci's horses or the *non finito* sculptures of Donatello.

Genius sputters and halts,
igniting cinder cones, incendiary sparks,
1775 thunderclaps and yellow booms,
intensity mercurial.

So white-hot, energy disintegrates its form,
manacles sawed through,
love—cracked and blistered,
God—death—gagged and tied.

Phasers set on "Stun"
or instant "Melody,"
beatific rainbows,
holocausts, gunpowder burns.

II

Yet can rape and shock
become so commonplace,
your mind so under siege,
the effect is almost nil?

1. Phrase taken from Emerson's poem "Merlin."

The dull *so-what?* of Bergen-Belsen,
another Allied carpet-bombing?
gulag after Siberian gulag,
Hiroshima followed by Nagasaki?

Might as well cap a gusher,
put a mafioso in his cage,
tie African elephants with silver knots,
as buckle Emily to a leash.

She shoots her popgun off at parties,
squirts your head with nitroglycerin,
like an Argonaut entices the golden fleece,
with St. George slays a grammarian dragon.

A hummingbird on a diet of saccharine
beats half as fast,
like the violent Thebans:
"On my volcano grows the Grass."

III

In fitful quirks of truth,
tossed out the foxglove's door,
the Mad Hatter of Amherst
composes baroque conceits.

Tremors of immortality—dashed,
twanged syllables, wormwood
mingled with the wine:
a new covenant of verse.

Master Donne Is Dead

The Exchequer of Death is done,
the Lord of Metaphysical Contortions
now finds himself on a missing foot,
that Champion of Christian Virtue
boldly tests his resurrection hypothesis,
that Prince of Divine Poets
has become jester and wit to discouraged angels.

Upon counting up unnumbered sins—
his island is now joined to that celestial Pangaea
from which we all once broke off,
surveying the damage done by this world's arch-barrister,
he holds conference with his pleading *gōʾêl*,
he who wrapped himself in Cicero's mantle
lives on in Scipio's dream.

How roughly Donne handled traditional rhyme,
choking the sonnet into an intense, more personal voice,
enticing the less than devout
by means of incongruities and outrageous first lines,
that Dantean celebrator of *amor*,
in all its earthly and uplifting forms,
broke ranks with the stiff Petrarchan mold.

His three-personed, ravished heart is
aglow with meditative song and the sweetest Anglican sentiments,
while his mind is attuned to the new science,

not buffeted by passing doubt,
his conceits bellow all over Europe
influencing a generation of florid, baroque imitators.

Let the Muses strew his casket with Easter lilies,
Erato pin a yew twig to his surplice-collar,
he who would preach by the hour-glass
on jubilant or melancholy themes
now converses with Moses, Elijah, and Paul,
yes, I can almost see his respectful, imposing figure
kneeling beside George Herbert and Jeremy Taylor.

Maybe there *Mermaides* are singing.

Angeli Domini

When they mount the Reformed pulpit,
do their words become the voice of God?
exegetical Luther, flowery Spurgeon,

graphic Whitefield, abstract Donne,
hurling invectives, cross-examining our conscience,
railing against Beelzebub, lifting us to a bronze serpent.

Leaky cups the potter toasts and ultimately discards,
effervescent, ecstatic, foaming over,
intoxicated with a brew patented by God.

Caress the Son through his intermediary,
jump the gap between momentary beads and *nunc stans*,
gravitate from righteousness to quintessential purity.

But as soon as they dismount
why call them father, reverend, priest or minister
—gullible, cranky, opinionated bards?

Lanterns eclipsed by the first thrust of dawn,
dry eddies inundated by a firmamental flood,
matchsticks consumed in the conflagration.

The Gospel reading rattles our smug one-liners,
the sermon pries into cardinal misdemeanor,
Charles Wesley opens up the bottle marked *Repentance*:

catharsis under the pseudonym of liturgy.

The lyre tames, the word takes root

in the brick and splintered glass of a faithless heart.

Haiku

I sample the haiku verses

as cherry blossoms blown down after a violent storm,

the skeins are moon-arc bright, though much-repeated,

the language is more painful than a samurai's sword

—I cut myself on the edges—

an unfamiliar tune drips down monotonously from the sandalwood
    samisen,

evanescent, unsculptured as a floating mood,

the crane's compression I admire, her buoyant, rhythmic feathers,

but I find myself overlooking the middle jewel,

(shall Kyoto commentators blather on longer than the seventeen
    original?)

indirectness either Rinzai shock-illuminates

or flails the turgid air,

courtesans may weep tears of flesh,

but I arise groping, blind as an obtuse apprentice.

In a Zen Rock Garden

Rivulets of sand course past the barren stone
where Hakuin and Dogen found *shibumi*,
water (gravel) falls, silica boats
on silica ponds, I think of green, a moment
like this should last forever, instead,
time's here by time betrayed.

Monochrome, no color,
like Rorschach's inky blots,
attachments and delusions I abhor,
bridges span swirling dry creek beds,
pebbles loom like towering Sung cliffs,
I turn my eyes from the stark, glaring waves.

Self, mind, world, Buddha
are as one, can interchange, reverse,
male and female merge and mesh,
my Eckhart! my Swedenborg! my Boehme!
to move the audience the players must
stand unmoved, oblivious to apparent change.

Buddhist Aesthetics

His foreshortened Pure Land goal—
a one-syllable
tanka poem.

My Mystic Eclogue

On warm afternoons
I take me out my telescope
for some uninhabited ridge,
there not to trouble heaven or mankind,
pick some muddleberries,
forget a while my duty,
flip colored balls to sapling tops,
whistle through the oats and alfalfa,
get me a little shut-eye.

The earth rumbles now and then
like a dream come quaking through,
I embroider and embellish
my mystic eclogue,
in this haven far from the bustle and traffic
I stretch and yawn—
assured that nothing substantial has blared,
Cupid carves his initials in my trunk.

I balk and lose control,
shiver near to an abyss,
swap themes, lisp in a foreign tongue—
this poem how unlike the Winding Water Banquet
or Ammons's adding-machine tapes,
Keats's contest for the finest cricket,
"Vulgar Superstition" produced in fifteen minutes
—chance compositions in blue-ribbon haste.

Spontaneous show-offs
who consecrate family heirlooms,
while I pluck living seed,
my voice rises in a premeditated fashion,
gay or austere, though conscious of its flight,
like a boiling teapot filled with facts,
I echo anthologies, hook allusions—
feeble flourishes with a palsied pen—
like a boy finding an abandoned shell on the beach
he makes his own.

The Garden of Hafiz

Here I sit
sipping my tea politely
in the garden of Hafiz,
hoping like any gravestone madman
to commune with Solomon.

A cup of rice for the nom de plume,
a chelo kebab for me,
like Saadi we know
the Muses squat on the cushions of their friends.

Perhaps I'll pilfer a thought or rhythm,
bowdlerize a mistranslated line,
Shakespeare had his Painter,
Pound his Chinaman,
Picasso's palette has been traced to *la pensée sauvage*.

I hope your roses, too,
will ferment inside my veins,
a touch of lyricism
to subdue my metaphysics.

Though I sacrifice my reputation,
you cower 'neath a purple blade,
afeared a fool eclectic
will forget to praise his source,
will absorb into his Hegel,
Demosthenes alongside little men.

Omnivorous Ameba

I inch forward like an omnivorous ameba,
enveloping and ingesting wholly
before I wiggle on.

The House of Memory

My mind is a house of memory,
in the basement I keep my fears,
in the bath I jettison my pride,
the bedroom is decorated with Kama Sutra kisses,
in the den I store my memorabilia
and oh so many snippets of my prose,
in the living room I seat my guests
and make small talk to my shelves,
the kitchen smells of gluttony,
in the attic are the cobwebs
and relics of my neuroses,
in the hall the children run their shuttle relays,
in the rec room I fabricate my legend,
in the storm cellar ideas ripen
and weather the critics' blasts,
while my garage takes me on adventures
my relatives could never fathom.

The windows are one-way mirrors,
the doors have their locks inside,
the shingles are eroded,
but the house only leaks when I'm mad,
the wooden panels are rotted
with evil inclinations,
and the walls are bent in upon themselves,
the stairs go from somewhere to nowhere,

and the banisters are remnants of comets' tails,
the furnace burnt out years ago
and I have no cascading stream of consciousness
—just pumps to prime.

A New Poet

We go to some new poet
thinking there to glimpse a portion
of our own unhindered beauty,
but from that self-flattering voyage,
our catch is woeful-thin.
I have a fine and concave mirror—
my wife and her tone-perfect ear.
What would Mr. Eliot do
were Ezra Pound cooing Imagist manifestoes
under his enervated Parisian sheets?
Move over, sassy Catullus.

Half My Life Is Over

Half my life is over,
half unspent,
dream-goals now seem remote, willowy,
others have been misshapen, twisted
out of Vitruvius proportion,
a few were too grandiose, immature
—I'm no Renaissance man.

II

Lucifer has built nests in my topmost branches,
cut away at my trunk, bored larva-like
through the woody xylem and phloem,
many diseased elms he's felled in a season,
his tent caterpillars have suffocated others,
my bark, like shingles, has fallen off and exposed the vulnerable
    heart,
I must bring this fellow low.

III

Thus far I've let others set their torrid pace,
not exhausting my limbs, nor appreciably closing the original gap,
exercising calm, disciplined restraint, not foolhardy lunges;
now, should determination prove strong and judgment correct,

I'll make my belated move,
pull out all stops, kick with a closing, last-minute flurry,
finish an increasingly strong contender, perhaps go for a crown.

Deeper Waters

I sit upon the misty beach,
can almost see from palm to hand,
the boats blend into chalky vapor
like the layers of a holograph.

Sparkling notions drench my head,
childhood pleasantries beat against my shore,
liquid thoughts revolve from turquoise to emerald,
gray to smoky yellow.
Who would have thought such dullness
could clear my circuit overload?

Imitating Descartes, I meditate on first principles:
a vocation, hobbies, dreams not yet realized,
a spitfire bride, doting kin,
second options one could still fall back on.

I ponder those infinite blue expanses
and the talus trail I leave behind.
Repairing my skiff, pulling up anchor,
trimming my sails—I head for deeper waters.

The Day the Muses Died

The day the Muses died
ice formed on my sombrero,
Thalia wore her dagger
and Erato's swan boat sank.

The creative juices soured vinegar,
the Castalian spring went underground,
Euterpe's flute filled up with gauze,
Urania's compass busted.

Like the dew the Israelites gathered
and Sol's torch blistered away,
or the time Campaspe giddy-upped on Aristotle,
my poetry stalemated.

Rhymes protruded like Eiffel Towers,
metaphors like Gothic cathedrals in Frank Lloyd Wright,
the old machinery hummed unerringly,
but the end product was a lemon.

My head swam in concentric circles
but with no red star to orbit,
I descended into Jeremiah's heart,
scrambled for Paul's *asoma* heaven.

I took off my shoes in an occultic gesture,
replaced my turban with Tom Terrific's cap,

like the wasp masturbated inside my favorite orchid,
zipped up my doors and windows—went fishin'.

There on the dirt road to Damascus pond
I was struck by Terpsichore's lightning,
my pastiche bait galvanized,
and I hauled up Calliope's trumpet.

Charms Which Wiggle

Indifferent to the world,
blinders to my right, blinders to my left,
I disregard idolatrous faces,
charms which wiggle, oxidize, and crumble,
Sirens that promise much and deliver precious little,
mountainous virtue commands my gaze
more than the compelling, grassy slopes of ease.

Fame is a passing, unreliable thing,
crowds bounce from Messiahs
like balls across a piddling net,
knights bow to their ladies,
are wounded, then taken to expire.

Fortune draws us to California's
magnetic shore, where we pan and shake,
suffer sunstroke, cough up more
for inflationary grub, should we strike a mother lode,
we've no contingency plans.

Beauty sings a familiar round,
puts on lotion and frosting make-up,
pads itself, then hopes for no gusts,
takes prizes, poses nude
before the wrinkles come.

The world hangs out its enticing shingle,
shopkeepers concoct elaborate window displays,
con-men scalp tickets, advertisers write blustery copy,
but I've pointed my head toward unseen pavilions
and the secret, unadorned beauty of inner character.

So-Called "Masterpieces"

Fluid memories keep pouring over my lukewarm life
so even so-called "masterpieces" take on a provisional score,
though sections of *Faust* are majestic and sublime,
Goethe reworks, perfects till the day of his death,
Van Gogh in Arles has hardly torn one vivid impression off his easel
before his unconscious sketches out another cross-pollinated by Gauguin,
such was the picnic those Siamese twins, Hawthorne and Melville, attended,
Picasso resembles Pound's incoming antenna
as the vanguard is continuously convulsed by stylistic coups d'état.

The Pythian oracle is mad when Apollo descends in a babbling frenzy—
such intoxicated poets could be banished from Plato's republic—
Blake and Li Po conversed intimately with otherworldly messengers,
John of Patmos was, at times, in the body,
at other times, lifted beyond the mystic, ungrammatical veil.
I, too, have been overtaken by poems walking through dreams,
half-awake, touched a brighter, purer world,
had my bowels torn, lacerated by a book, a chance conversation, a simple
     nature reverie,
till a decanter of Gaelic fairies ran up and down my vertebrae.

But the usual prescription is to gut it out at my desk,
here an allusion, there a visual stroke, maybe a neo-startling, symbolic cluster,
perhaps a rhythmic, ear-perfect, atonal line,
the introduction's fine, the body sprawls, but I can't put pizzazz in the finale,
or the images are sufficiently consistent, but sadly unmemorable,
or so far-out and rudely juxtaposed that the result is idiosyncratic,

or there's an ignited flash of memory, but the narrative proves unhistorical;
I can paper over all with disclaimers of poetic license
or start from scratch to recapture a truer picture of my original point of view.

Like Edison who threw out 99 filaments for one incandescent bulb,
some—who are talented—seek peak, otherworldly experiences,
while my Christ lies buried deep within,
and there, beholding his hidden face, I am little by little reinvigorated,
    transmogrified.

Tradition

Tradition weighs me down
like a cord of miracles
makes the devil believe,
my predecessors are so eccentric
I want to build a new, evangelical church.

My genetic tissue is overlaid
with Belgian *paterfamilias*,
my upbringing stamped in loam,
when empathetic awareness is required,
once more in Adam I'm retroactive.

One hundred joints, nine openings,
six organs—all coalesce to form my body—
a stout heart, a flabby torso,
blue chip memory circuits,
Iowa's own pragmatic hands.

Like a bladder unrelieved I burst,
damn my Irish temper,
I mock my backwash Protestant ways,
lacking innate genius,
perhaps imitation will coax me to verse.

Home

If ever I return to earth
I shall walk down this lane again,
nodding to old acquaintances,
ducking thrown balls and paper kites,
admiring the purple and jostled green,
eyeing the hems of swaying skirts.

When I walk, it shall be with the ether of perfume,
my simple khaki shirt,
I'll salute the sycamore and the grunting hog,
whistle a Tom Sawyer-Huck Finn medley,
half-incarnate, half-disembodied,
my joy like Wordsworth's will know no bounds.

I'll weave through the crab apple and daffodil,
a gorgeous sunflower cranes its neck,
in the pasture our pontoon bridge,
I'll be intoxicant of the open air.

There's mom hanging out towels,
dad shelling, grinding, cultivating,
my brother and I coming home from school,
sis has her dolls to tea.

Thus far have I come
and still my throat constricts,
on the mind's supersaturate canvas
appear all who meant so much to me.

This Sleepy Town

What shall stir this sleepy town?
a smut tabloid, a tornado, political infighting,
news of the gold standard's demise, a veteran killed in action,
some hometown lad made good.

Surely not my groping for lyrical precision
nor the silent chemistry of ideas percolating;
a TV star, a jazz musician,
a new-fangled brand of ice cream—success of any kind—
will win their ephemeral applause and admiration.

But far from the chattering primates,
where mass values are stamped and embossed,
I'll embroider my twice-told tales
into ivory and gold; perchance some antique collector
will discover and promote their worth.

Why Doesn't the World Celebrate Quality?

Why doesn't the world celebrate quality?
    stubs her toe on genius,
    lynches her prophets,
    worships at Kitsch's feet.

Embalms her poets in a gilded cage,
    why don't her corks bob
    and pull up a saintly fish?
    instead she throws up crystalline arches from neo-derivatives.

Like Kiyoyuki all commune via Chinese dreams,
    or like bellwether New Hampshire
    we lie prostrate before a mass-man king,
    a crayon-smeared paper doll, Madison Avenue sublimate.

A Mirror with a Memory

I've a mirror with a memory
and rolls and rolls of unexposed film—
some to preserve my dear children in,
towns we've visited,
exuberant local celebrations.

People who walk in and out of life
return in black-and-white vignettes
or a visual diary of yellowing daguerreotypes.

Here's where I proposed,
the unknown relatives who attended grandpa's funeral,
our hurricane weekend at the cape,
the time we got lost at Mount Tom,
little Ken's tooth came screaming through.

In the scraps, snippets, and bluing colors
lie archives of spontaneous truth
long forgotten by winded orators and pedantic commentators.

The day our Ford blew up,
the first recital of our piano daughter's,
that lantern kite which never got off the ground,
a restaurant where Bangladeshi waiters kept dropping cups,
swapping tips, bringing in Urdu menus.

Snapshots from a feature-length film;
beneath the incandescent glare
unknowns are cast as screen sensations.

There's the Halloween costume composed of silk balloons,
our horseshoe pitching contest behind the barn,
a soiled picnic at marvelous pond,
graduations, weddings, birthdays, anniversaries, christenings,
my right arm in a sling, our rebuilt porch.

It's in our leisure that we're most revealed,
fully captured by inverse light:
in glossy prints more valuable than goblets of tourmaline.

I Felt a Smile . . .

I felt a smile
run down my cheeks
like a clown looking
for his lost laugh,
after years of preparation
I lapsed in my sleight of hand.

Was it a converse fluke?
or merely rusty fingers?
did my audience notice?
see my embarrassed mouth?

I went "on with the show"
like good performers do
with quips and the usual one-liners,
the applause detonated,
my timing improved,
the manager granted a raise.

Yet will historians record this—
the beginning of my demise?

Misguided Muses

Some critics urge me to dredge
deeper and broader channels,
but I go back to the same sinkholes for inspiration,
at my age
there's little hope for another, more revelatory mentor,
I tap water from flowing artesian wells.

Other poets paste together flash-card verse,
settle into stodgy Victorian modes
or have an archaeological interest
in *uta*, *terza rima*, old Saxon declensions
or cramp their innovative vistas
into miniature symbolist paintings.

For a few, the unconscious free-sprawls
in paltry chuckles and a box of sardonic delicacies,
but they've sold their coat of many colors for beatnik rags
because they're not steeped in the dense,
resonating tones of the symphonic classics,
even romantic Keats traced his etchings off Attic vases.

I, too, wander about Greek isles and Semitic lands,
mellifluous compositions outside the orthodox Occidental fold,
try out newfangled consonants, cuneiform, mantras
drawn from the recesses of the scattered Vedic soul;
my chief problem is that the Muses
have a weak, dilatory, un-epic attention span.

Editors

Pencil-pushing fools,
afraid their jobs
depend on a quota of crossed-out lines,
seek to lasso talent
into familiar grooves,
throw up their hands
at an obsolescent word,
gaze in anguish
at convoluted syntax,
squeamish before
a decades-old controversy,
dredge out thoroughfares
for inconspicuous digressions.

Salaried by marketeers,
cushioned so as not to provoke,
search and destroy
the extraordinary,
marvelous imprecision.
Rate comma above
edifying quotation,
style book
before the bard himself,
you jot and tittle scribes.

How much English prose
has been decimated by poor judgment,
milquetoast-authors crippled
by pig-headed mules,
appointed midwives who
become mercy killers?

I know! All my life
they've wrung
this bone-dry rag
or used it for target practice,
set me back 3-to-5 years
out of envy.
Rewarded by also-rans,
they call "success"
the criterion of the Muse.

Engulf me? change my thesis?
a title, sure—
but a new introduction *and* conclusion—
what's left?
My name is on the piece,
not yours,
Egomaniacal Bureaucrat.
Oh, distance yourself,
I'm comin' through.

A Reviewer's Dispute

You think it hilarious,
I find it appalling,
you're aglow with "How seminal! Profound!"
I blather out, "How stupid! Inane!"
you resort to Pindaric odes,
I'm inclined more to jeremiads,
you quote "lustrous" paragraphs whole,
I'm befuddled diagramming the ungrammatical locutions.

You espouse, "These sentiments are fit for the ages,"
I consider them "compost for my garden,"
you compare the style to Virgil, Dante, and Homer,
I wouldn't insult my most vulgar contemporary . . .
you demand four-color fold-out spreads,
I prefer typeface in the shape of a tombstone.

You're anxious to cast the maxims in monumental brass,
I'm hoping some new Savonarola will ignite a bonfire of vanities,
you believe the whole "nuanced, drenched with originality,"
I inquire if it wasn't cribbed off the Internet,
you're eager to pass on the flame as a baton,
while I'd like to turn on my hose to douse any leftover embers.

You demand a Nobel (or at least a Pulitzer),
I'm more sympathetic to the pillory and a flogging,
now I wonder, "Have we both read the same proofs?
Again, how are you spelling the name?"

To Avoid Criticism

To avoid criticism:
make melody to the deaf,
perform acrobatics before the blind,
carry on conversation with the dumb,
then clap loudly and whistle as you bow.

Ennui

This poem bores me now,
line follows line
with disconcerting ease,
as if passion could be carved
out of vacant thought:
innocuous, syrupy phrases,
greeting card platitudes,
satiric couplets pinched from Pope.

I throttle a valve in my unconscious,
spout clichés and advertisements
till it makes me yawn,
friends rave, critics hand in
their glittering superlatives,
awards come flocking in like migrating ducks.
So what? I've pushed on in nearly a hundred new directions
and couldn't care less what they think of the old.

The Wreck of My Own Self

Leaning against the wind,
invigorated by a head-on gale,
like a penguin waddling across the equator
or an owl scout-hooting at high noon,
I bend my technological/management
potential into nectar for Erato.
It's far too easy to repeat
a successful parent's song and dance,
form partnerships with relatives kind,
refurbish an ancestral house,
make a coterie of friends of similar class,
hew talents into a display case
of trophies: "Individual" or "Family" Achievement.

But I've chosen the windward side,
the serpentine path that cloaks
brambles, repetitious curves, entangling loops;
I've almost flunked rhetoric,
been told my vocabulary was
not quite accurate; red-marked by
the traditional, sneered, scoffed at
by the avant-garde, I've grown
accustomed to dismissal, start to
doubt all honest praise,
find myself a recluse, evading even
the opportunities I once had sought.

Wavering on the periphery, my
boat capsizes; all hands are lost,
presumed dead; divers, however,
locate an archival bonanza,
while a few old teachers weep.

To Know God's Will

To know God's will is a wearisome proposition:
what task to perform?
which guests to entertain?
even which enchanting woman to wed?

Pray stop. Pray advance.
politeness could hold this door open for hours,
how should I show love to a neighbor—
through greater intimacy or by leaving well enough alone?
how do the Ten Commandments
impinge on my choice of leisure?
what percentage of my income should I save or give away?

Of these two vocations:
which has more potential for service,
can take advantage of my mediocre talents?
in other words, should I stretch or relax?
how much time ought I to set aside for solitude, introspection,
and how much for public weal?
is it better to pardon or punish the offender,
forgive the ne'er-do-well?

What can foster independence, growth,
yet still keep a child's evil proclivities under control?
should I hold on tight or cut the string,
allow for flops and miscues?

trust to intuition
or defer to an outside panel of experts?
labor or pray?

Is my life cruciform balanced or woefully misshaped?
satisfactory solutions are only intermittently illumined this side of
    the grave.

The Prodigal Philosopher

Plotinus contemplating the One,
St. Francis preaching to the birds,
Christ crucified,
and me backing into eternity.

Three times I asked my Lord for faith
that I might say to that obstacle,
"Begone you superego fantasy."
For Max Weber was my hero
and Sisyphus my bête noire,
as if I could storm the kingdom
by means of prayer, memorization, and alms.
In my youth, plums were for the asking
and snakes . . . afraid of trees.

But when maturity came
I believed faith more for children.
So God, said I, make great books my master,
construct skyscrapers impervious to change,
make me the Newton of flux,
unlike Tertullian: *credo quia absurdum.*
But young Schiller pulled out my cornerstone,
lifelong edifices crumbled with one blow,
MENE, MENE, TEKEL and *PARSIN.*

So tired and senile I returned,
the upstart prodigal philosopher,
desired a few more years of faith,
but thought my request impertinent;
instead, He remembered me.
I whispered repentance to all my friends,
prayed up a storm in my rocking chair,
like Methuselah exhibited shadings of grace and peace:
"While others grow cranky, rigid, and closed,
now you, the latecomer, serve me more than they."

Apologetics

What would it take, Voltaire,
to turn your satire into praise,
your witty barbs into Dantean comedy?

What would you require, Maimonides,
to cause your piety to become love,
your learned exegesis, Messianic allegory?

What Sanctus might you hum, Bertrand Russell,
to make your agnosticism unpeel,
your logical atomism, Augustinian metaphysics?

What argument would win you over, Celsus,
enough to bow before a Jewish king,
your aristocratic pride accept humility?

What of you, dear reader,
how could your doubt revert to faith,
if not by my reprehensible lines, perhaps another's?

A Legacy

Let me gather what remains of this world's goods
to bequeath an ounce of happiness
to those I leave behind.

My days have scurried on like the sundial's inching hand,
most in self-absorption,
a beggarly few by love redeemed.

My talents, a happy groove discovered,
whether or no posterity be blessed,
a choleric disposition buoyed by a palmer's branch.

As to structural flaws—please be kind,
and experiments that failed, remember, from a dead pond a bog is
     made;
pernicious notions are myopically Mine not his.

For those who wished he'd stayed a farmer,
in a pre-industrial age perhaps he could,
but a wee bit of education sucked him like Ulysses's siren.

Here at Life's End

Temptations are placid and cool,
my will needs rewording,
my enemies forgiving,
a few outstanding bills should be paid,
I owe thank-yous to friends
who believed me capable
of greater things, my wife deserves
a nest egg—in case of hospitalization.

The last poems I wrote require a surgeon's hand,
several choice aphorisms should close
my collected works, making more frequent reference
to obscurer sources might save a biographer
embarrassment, I'll lay to rest one or two
unmitigated controversies, patch up rifts
due to obstinacy and rancor,
urge contemporaries to follow a private muse.

    Yet to some extent
    I feel content, though
    I've lived far differently
    than I imagined
    as a boy—I suppose
    my personality's about
    the same—still quiet,
    studious, conscientious.

But my scope has engulfed
cultures myriad. I've
been admired, stretched
the tendons in my head,
had people ask for my opinion,
I was the exemplar, pace-setting
good fellow, though minorities
might harpoon my insensitivities.

My talents were not those of an earth-shaker,
if I had lived in a totalitarian state
courage and conviction might have rewritten
the backdrop to my tears. Or born a few
decades earlier in this paranoiac century,
I'd be buried in a Flanders poppy plot.
As it is, I've had the good fortune of old age,
bounteous health and mere rumors of war.

Send for the priest, anoint
my ears, eyes, and nose, *sacramentum
exeuntium* and I'll be goin',
glad for my pleasant stay, hopeful
my art will both instruct and amuse,
critics will cauterize my wounds,
this race will move on to heights,
feats unfathomed, undreamed.

Then think of me in my wheelchair,
your uncle, clappin',
cheerin' you on your way.

An Epilogue

The life is not
consistent with this poem,
with itself,
with assorted theoretical pronouncements,
or even the sympathetic biographer,
for an ineradicable fog
enshrouds the pulmonary aorta.

"As I Crossed a Bridge of Dreams"[2]

As I crossed a bridge of dreams
a phoenix and a dove appeared,
ripples of sorrow crushed my chest,
    like a surrealistic film:
        bodies floated,
    ibises gorged on serpents,
    Freudian keyholes opened
        like a moistened vulva.

From the unfathomed deep, forgotten labyrinths,
medicine men and minstrels string together tales,
between my blanket and my pillow, childhood alchemy.

    Shaping and reshaping myth
    in this self-collapsing universe,
    I Marco-Polo enter the Forbidden City
    with ground-up dragon bones my aphrodisiac.

Color is form,
the subconscious gives it shape,
substance is immaterial,
the essence almost void,
Photuris flashes *Photinus*.

Why are there no pure red flowers,
you colorblind bees?
what became of the Apatosaurus

2. Title taken from a Japanese diary translated by Ivan Morris.

or what of the mass extinction in the Mesozoic Age?
the boundary between soul and spirit?
pulsating gravitons?
the "madder" family of flowers?

In Byzantium lions roar, artificial nightingales sing,
in the Land of the Rising Sun dwells the noble cat Lady Myobu,
according to Gamaliel, in the Messianic era
women will bear children like hens lay eggs . . .

I live in Celtic twilight,
a half-converted soul,
responsible for my actions,
lost in nightmares and dreams.

Recommended Reading on Creativity

Bauer, Michael J. *Arts Ministry: Nurturing the Creative Life of God's People.* Grand Rapids: Eerdmans, 2013.

Csikszentmihalyi, Mihaly. *Creativity: Flow and the Psychology of Discovery and Invention.* New York: HarperCollins, 1996.

Daniel J. Boorstin. *The Creators: A History of Heroes of the Imagination.* New York: Vintage, 1993.

Eco, Umberto. *Art and Beauty in the Middle Ages.* Translated by Hugh Bredin. New Haven: Yale University Press, 1986.

Eliot, T.S. *Four Quartets.* New York: Harcourt, Brace and World, 1971.

Ghiselin, Brewster, ed. *The Creative Process: A Symposium.* New York: New American Library, 1963.

Glaspey, Terry. *75 Masterpieces Every Christian Should Know.* Grand Rapids: Baker, 2015.

Harries, Richard. *Art and the Beauty of God: A Christian Understanding.* London: Mowbray, 1994.

Hazelton, Roger. *A Theological Approach to Art.* Nashville: Abingdon, 1967.

Koestler, Arthur. *The Act of Creation: A Story of the Conscious and Unconscious in Science and Art.* New York: Dell, 1967.

L'Engle, Madeleine. *Walking on Water: Reflections on Faith and Art.* New York: Farrar, Straus and Giroux, 1995.

Maritain, Jacques. *Creative Intuition in Art and Poetry.* New York: Meridian, 1955.

O'Connor, Flannery. *Mystery and Manners: Occasional Prose.* Selected and edited by Sally and Robert Fitzgerald. New York: Farrar, Straus and Giroux, 1979.

Ryken, Leland, ed. *The Christian Imagination.* Revised and expanded edition. Colorado Springs: Shaw Books, 2002.

Sayers, Dorothy L. *The Mind of the Maker.* New York: Meridian, 1956.

Thiessen, Gesa Elsbeth, ed. *Theological Aesthetics: A Reader.* Grand Rapids: Eerdmans, 2004.

Wittkower, Rudolf and Margot. *Born Under Saturn: The Character and Conduct of Artists.* New York: Norton, 1969.

Listing of Photographs

1. Boy with open mouth in mirror [A Whisper]

2. Jewish cemetery in Manhattan [Have Done with Donne]

3. Queen statue pondering [A Minor Manifesto]

4. Horse and carriage conveying riders in Central Park [The Land of Make-Believe]

5. Young man writing on tablet [Poetic Diction]

6. Male and female marionettes [Pretend]

7. Actor and nearby shadow of a hand [In the Circle of Light]

8. Street vendor in cowboy outfit [*Homo Hypocrites*]

9. Dwarf statue and unicorn in window [In the Middle, Fabulous Kingdom]

10. Reflection of flowers above white bed [The Glass Flowers]

11. Decorative light in Lincoln Center [Miniature Illusions]

12. Man sitting in chair [A Surrealist's Manifesto]

13. People on moving carousel [A Futurist Declaration]

14. Shaker spiral staircase ["Stairway of Surprise"]

15. Hand holding cross in metal candelabrum [Master Donne Is Dead]

16. Episcopal church at Jersey shore [*Angeli Domini*]

17. Barley in field [My Mystic Eclogue]

18. Old house with torn screens [The House of Memory]

Works Cited

Auden, W.H. "For the Time Being: A Christmas Oratorio." In *Religious Drama 1: Five Plays*, edited by Marvin Halverson, 11–68. New York: Meridian, 1960.

Saint Augustine. *On Genesis*. Translated by Edmund Hill, edited by John E. Rotelle. Hyde Park: New City Press, 2001.

Bauer, Michael J. *Arts Ministry: Nurturing the Creative Life of God's People*. Grand Rapids: Eerdmans, 2013.

Blumhardt, Christoph. *Action in Waiting*. Farmington, PA: Plough, 1998.

Canfield, Dorothy. "How 'Flint and Fire' Started and Grew." In *Americans All: Stories of American Life of To-day*, edited by Benjamin A. Heydrick, 210–20. New York: Harcourt, Brace and Company, 1921.

Charley, J.W. "Deism." In *The New International Dictionary of the Christian Church*. Revised edition, edited by J.D. Douglas, 290. Grand Rapids: Zondervan, 1978.

Clement, Clara Erskine. *Charlotte Cushman*. Boston: James R. Osgood, 1882.

Gerard, R.W. "The Biological Basis of Imagination." In *The Creative Process: A Symposium*, edited by Brewster Ghiselin, 226–51. New York: New American Library, 1963.

Hazelton, Roger. *A Theological Approach to Art*. Nashville: Abingdon, 1967.

Hendrickson, Robert. *The Facts on File Encyclopedia of Word and Phrase Origins*. New York: Facts on File, 1987.

Hill, Jonathan. *The History of Christian Thought*. Downers Grove, IL: InterVarsity, 2003.

Holt, Jim. *Why Does the World Exist?* New York: Liveright, 2013.

Irenaeus. "Against Heresies." In *The Ante-Nicene Fathers, Volume 1*, edited by Alexander Roberts and James Donaldson, 309–567. New York: Charles Scribner's Sons, 1903.

James, Henry. "Preface to *The Spoils of Poynton*." In *Theory of Fiction: Henry James*, edited by James E. Miller Jr., 71–73. Lincoln: University of Nebraska Press, 1972.

James, William. *Some Problems of Philosophy*. New York: Longmans, Green, and Co., 1911.

Kołakowski, Leszek. *Why Is There Something Rather Than Nothing? 23 Questions from Great Philosophers*. Translated by Agnieszka Kołakowska. New York: Basic, 2007.

Lewis, C.S. *The Magician's Nephew*. New York: HarperCollins, 1983.

Lossky, Vladimir. *The Mystical Theology of the Eastern Church*. Crestwood, NY: St. Vladimir's Seminary Press, 1976.

Mozart, Wolfgang Amadeus. "A Letter." In *Creativity: Selected Readings*, edited by P.E. Vernon, 55–56. New York: Penguin, 1976.

Newton, A. Edward. *The Amenities of Book-Collecting and Kindred Affections*. Boston: Atlantic Monthly Press, 1918.

Parkinson, G.H.R, ed. *Leibniz: Philosophical Writings*. Translated by Mary Morris and G.H.R. Parkinson. London: J.M. Dent & Sons, 1977.

Pater, Walter. "Conclusion to *Studies in the History of the Renaissance*." In *Literary Criticism: Pope to Croce*, edited by Gay Wilson Allen and Harry Hayden Clark, 526–30. Detroit: Wayne State University Press, 1962.

Pater, Walter. *Studies in the History of the Renaissance*. New York: Oxford University Press, 2010.

Pickering, James S. *Captives of the Sun*. New York: Dodd, Mead & Company, 1961.

Polkinghorne, John. *The Faith of a Physicist: Reflections of a Bottom-Up Thinker*. Minneapolis: Fortress, 1996.

Rahner, Karl. *Theological Investigations, Volume IV: More Recent Writings*. Translated by Kevin Smyth. London: Darton, Longman & Todd, 1966.

Rilke, Rainer Maria. "Brief 4." In *Briefe an einen jungen Dichter*. Leipzig: Hythloday Press, 2004.

Rilke, Rainer Maria. *Letters to a Young Poet*. Revised edition. Translated by M.D. Herter Norton. New York: Norton, 1962.

Sayers, Dorothy L. *Gaudy Night*. New York: HarperCollins, 2012.

Sayers, Dorothy L. *The Mind of the Maker*. New York: Meridian, 1956.

Shaw, Luci. "Beauty and the Creative Impulse." In *The Christian Imagination*. Revised and expanded edition, edited by Leland Ryken, 81–99. Colorado Springs: Shaw Books, 2001.

Spender, Stephen. "The Making of a Poem." In *The Creative Process: A Symposium*, edited by Brewster Ghiselin, 112–25. New York: New American Library, 1963.

Stringham, Edwin John. *Listening to Music Creatively*. 2d ed. Englewood Cliffs, NJ: Prentice-Hall, 1959.

Underhill, Evelyn. *Mysticism*. New York: New American Library, 1955.

Vahanian, Gabriel. *Wait Without Idols*. New York: George Braziller, 1964.